STEVE PARISH
BIG
Picture Book of
AUSTRALIAN
RAINFOREST

PHOTOGRAPHS BY STEVE PARISH

WORDS BY PAT SLATER

AUSTRALIAN RAINFORESTS

Rainforests grow where there is plenty of rain. Australia has different sorts of rainforest, some growing in warm places, others growing in cool places. These damp green rainforests are homes to fascinating animals and plants. Once there were large stands of rainforest on Australia's eastern side. Today a lot of this forest has been chopped down, and many rainforest animals have become rare. Many people are trying to save rainforest and its animals.

▲ *The Red-eyed Tree-frog lives in the tops of forest trees*

BOWERBIRDS

A bower is a kind of building which has plants all around it. The male bowerbird builds a bower of twigs on the forest floor. Some bowerbirds paint their bowers with juices they crush from plants. A male bowerbird collects treasures, such as berries, bones and glass, then places them around the bower. When a female comes, he sings and dances for her and shows her his treasures. If she likes him, she mates with him, then flies away and builds a nest. She looks after the eggs and chicks all by herself.

STANLEY BREEDEN

▲
Male Regent Bowerbird

▶ *Male Satin Bowerbird adding a stick to his bower*

M & I MORCOMBE

▲ *The male Golden Bowerbird decorates his bower with lichen*

▲ *Grey-headed Robin*　　▲ *Flame Robin*　　▶ *Eastern Yellow Robin*

ROBINS

Australia's robins are small plump birds, which often sing at dawn. Some sorts of robins live in the rainforest, where they catch insects to eat. In springtime, a pair of robins will choose a safe place to build a nest, which they make from strips of bark, bits of creepers and cobwebs. Many robins put small pieces of green lichen or bark on the outsides of their nests. While the female robin sits on the eggs, the male brings her food. When the chicks hatch, both parents feed them on insects.

DRAGONS

▲
Boyd's Forest Dragon

STANLEY BREEDEN

Dragons are lizards which have strong legs and can run fast. They have long tails and some have crests of large scales on their necks and down their backs. All dragons eat small animals such as insects. Rainforest dragons hide from their enemies on tree trunks. They can change their colour so their skins look like bark and their crests look like lichen or moss. If an enemy comes close, a dragon clinging to a tree moves to the other side of the trunk. Several female dragons may lay their eggs together in a nest in an earth bank.

▶ *Southern Forest Dragon on a tree trunk*

▲ *Southern Forest Dragon*

8

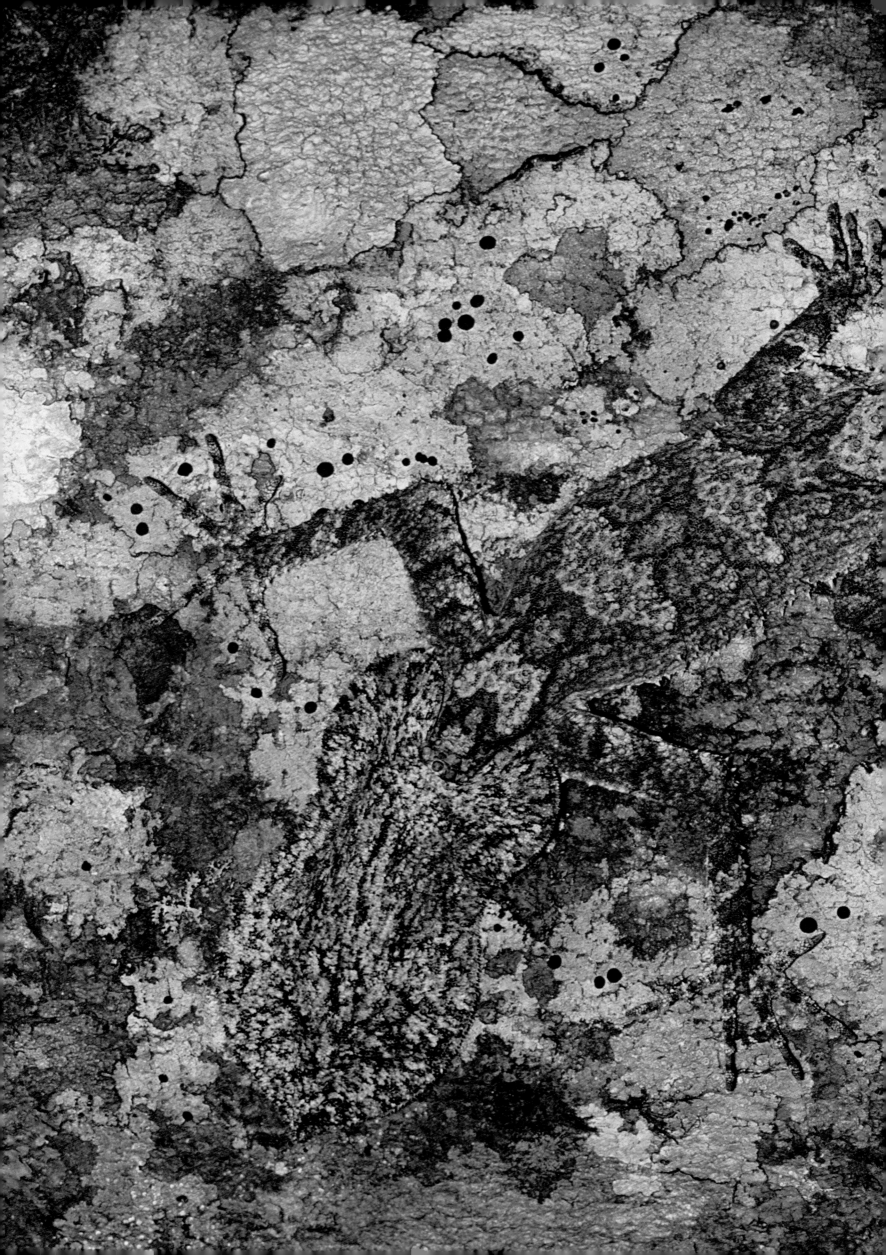

GECKOS

Geckos are lizards with soft skins and big eyes. Since they have no eyelids, they use their tongues to lick dirt from their eyes. Geckos eat insects and other small animals. Some geckos have pads on their fingers and toes, which cling onto bark and stone when the geckos climb. The skin of the Leaf-tailed Gecko looks like bark covered with lichen, so it hides from its enemies by staying very still on a branch.

STANLEY BREEDEN

◀ *Leaf-tailed Gecko*　　　　▲ *Ringtailed Gecko*

▲ *Stag beetle*   ▶ *Jewel bugs*   ▲ *Jewel beetle*

BUGS AND BEETLES

Bugs and beetles are insects. All insects have six legs and their bodies are divided into three parts, head, thorax and abdomen. A bug has a beak, which it stabs into a plant or animal then sucks up the juices. A beetle has jaws and chews its food. Bugs hatch from their eggs as small copies of adult bugs. Beetles hatch as grubs, which grow, then change into adult beetles.

BUTTER

▲
*Ulysses
Butterfly*

▲
*Cairns
Birdwing
Butterfly*

Butterflies are insects. A butterfly's
feelers end in little knobs. It flies around
during daytime and sucks nectar from
flowers. Some male butterflies have their
own home territories and fly in a special
way to attract females. After mating,
a female butterfly lays eggs. Each egg
hatches into a caterpillar, which eats
leaves. When it has grown big enough,
it changes into a pupa, which rests inside
a pupal case, changing into a butterfly.
The case splits and the butterfly comes
out. After its wings have grown to their
full size and dried, the lovely insect
flies away.

▶ *Leafwing Butterfly*

▲ *Union Jack Butterflies on pupal cases*

14

BIRDS WITH

▲ *Eastern Whipbird feeding chicks* ▶ *Green Catbird*

M & I MORCOMBE

Birds make their calls for different reasons. Many birds sing loudly to warn other birds to stay away from their home territories. The whipbird does this with a whip-crack call. Sometimes a bird calls to say it is looking for a mate. The male lyrebird mimics the songs of other birds, as well as singing its own song, when trying to attract a female. The male catbird makes a call that sounds like a cat meowing. A bird may make loud alarm calls that warn other birds that it can see an enemy, such as a snake.

▲ *Male Superb Lyrebird*

LOUD VOICES

ECLECTUS

When a rainforest tree carries fruit, birds gather to feast. Eclectus Parrots are among the colourful parrots which live in the forest. Like all parrots, they have two toes on each foot pointing forwards and two pointing backwards and they sometimes hold food in one foot while they eat it. The male Eclectus Parrot shown below is preening its feathers with its beak. Preening keeps a bird's feathers tidy and well-groomed so it can fly well.

▲ *Male Eclectus Parrot preening*   ▶ *Female Eclectus Parrot*

PARROT

FLYING-FOX

▲ *Grey-headed Flying-fox*　▶ *Spectacled Flying-fox getting ready to fly*

Flying-foxes are big bats, which fly on wings of thin skin joining their fingers and their legs. Mobs of flying-foxes spend the day hanging upside down by their feet in trees. At night they fly off to find rainforest flowers and fruit to eat. They may have to travel a long way to find their food, then fly all the way back to their camp by dawn.

PIGEONS

Fruit-eating pigeons like the Topknot Pigeon fly in flocks between stands of forest looking for food, then feed in the tree-tops. The Emerald Dove and the Wonga Pigeon waddle around the forest edges, feeding on fruits which have fallen to the ground. A pair of pigeons will build a flimsy nest of thin sticks in a tree. The female lays two white eggs, then she and her mate incubate them. When a chick hatches, it begs for food. A parent takes the chick's beak into its own beak, then pumps a special food called pigeon's milk into the chick's throat. Later the chick is fed on fruit.

▲
Wonga Pigeon

PETER SLATER

▲ *Emerald Dove*　　　　　　　　　▶ *Topknot Pigeon*

22

TURTLES

Rainforest rivers and streams are home to freshwater turtles. A turtle's body is hidden in a shell. Some turtles have short necks and can pull their heads between the edges of their hard shells. Other turtles with long necks find it hard to hide their heads between their shells. Turtles swim with webbed feet and eat animals they catch in the water. Sometimes a turtle lies on a log or on the bank near the water, warming itself in the sunshine.

IAN MORRIS

◄ *A short-necked turtle*   ▲ *Eastern Long-necked Turtle*

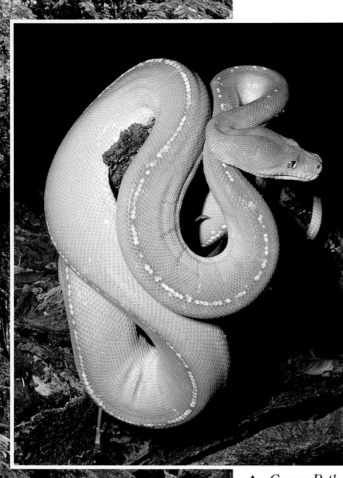

▲ *Green Python*   ▲ *Carpet Python*   ▶ *Diamond Python tasting the air*

PYTHONS

Pythons are snakes with strong, muscular bodies. When a python is hungry, it flicks out its forked tongue, tastes the scent an animal has left behind and follows it. Little pits on the python's face track the heat given out by the animal's body. A python does not have poison fangs, so after it grabs the animal with its mouth it coils around it and squeezes it so it cannot breathe. Then it opens its mouth wide and swallows the dead animal. Farmers like pythons in their sheds because they eat rats and mice.

FROGS

STANLEY BREEDEN

▲ *Male frog calling*   ▲ *Green Tree-frog*

Frogs have soft moist skins and live in damp places. When a male frog calls for a mate, he puffs out his throat. After frogs mate, their eggs hatch into tadpoles, which grow into adult frogs. Many rainforest frogs have discs on their fingers and toes. These discs help them hold onto leaves and bark.

▲ *Dainty Green Tree-frog calling for a mate*   ▶ *Red-eyed Tree-frog*

FRESHWATER

▲ *River Murray Cray*　▶ *Blue Lamington Cray*

Crays are related to crabs and
prawns. They have hard body
armour and ten legs, the first
pair ending in big claws. The
eyes of crays are on moveable
stalks and they touch things
with their long feelers to find
out about them. The Blue
Lamington Cray may leave
the stream it lives in and
crawl over the forest floor.
If it feels it is in danger, the
cray makes a loud hissing
noise and waves its claws
to scare off the enemy.

CRAYS

CASSOWARY

The Southern Cassowary is a big rainforest bird which cannot fly. It has bright blue bare skin and two red wattles on its neck and on its head is a bony crest called a casque. The hole behind a cassowary's eye is the opening to its ear. After the female cassowary lays her eggs, she goes away and the male sits on them. When the eggs hatch, he looks after the striped chicks, showing them where to find fruit to eat and protecting them from enemies.

▲ *Southern Cassowary*

STANLEY BREEDEN

STANLEY BREEDEN

▲ *Male Southern Cassowary with chicks*

▶ *The cassowary has strong legs and feet*

POSSUMS

▲ *Northern Ringtail Possum*

STANLEY BREEDEN

Possums and cuscuses are furry animals which feed their babies on milk. They are marsupials, whose young ones are born too early to survive away from their mothers' bodies and spend the first part of their lives in their mothers' pouches. Possums climb trees and most of them eat leaves and fruit at night. Ringtail possums can hold onto branches with their strong, curling tails. The Striped Possum, which eats insects, cannot hold branches with its tail, but it is good at jumping between trees. The fur of the Green Ringtail Possum is the same colour as the bark and lichen of the rainforest.

▶ *Green Ringtail Possum*

STANLEY BREEDEN

STANLEY BREEDEN

▲ *Striped Possum*　　　▲ *Daintree River Ringtail Possum*

Following pages: Spotted Cuscus (STANLEY BREEDEN)

KINGFISHERS

Kingfishers have big heads and long sharp beaks. Their feathers are often brightly coloured in shades of blue and green. The Azure Kingfisher lives near a rainforest stream and has a favourite perch over the water from which it dives to catch yabbies, frogs and fish. It nests in a burrow in the river bank. The Buff-breasted Paradise-Kingfisher digs its nest hole into a low mound built by termites on the ground and feeds its chicks insects and snails. The long white tailfeathers which stream behind it seem very bright in the dark rainforest.

▲ *Azure Kingfisher with a yabbie* ▶ *Buff-breasted Paradise-Kingfisher*

KANGAROOS
WALLABIES

STANLEY BREEDEN

▲ *Musky Rat-kangaroo*   ▶ *Bennett's Wallaby with young one in her pouch*

IAN MORRIS

▲ *Lumholtz's Tree-kangaroo*

Several members of the kangaroo family live in rainforest. The tiny Musky Rat-kangaroo is the smallest kangaroo of all. It does not hop on its hind legs like other kangaroos but bounds and carries leaves in its tail to build a nest. Tree-kangaroos have strong legs and the soles of their feet are covered with bumps which give a grip on bark. Bennett's Wallaby lives in cold Tasmanian rainforest, where its thick fur keeps it warm.

AND

OWLS

Owls hunt for small animals at night, both in the rainforest and along its edges where it joins other more open sorts of forest. Because their flight feathers have soft fluffy edges, owls make no sound when hunting. They can see in very dim light and their good hearing allows them to find prey just by tracking the noise it makes. Owls lay their white eggs in hollows in trees. Australia has two different sorts of owls. A hawk owl has a separate circle of feathers around each eye. A barn owl's eyes are set in a heart-shaped disc of feathers.

▲ *Young Rufous Owl*   ▲ *Masked Owl*   ▶ *Boobook Owl*

PLATYPUS

The Platypus lives in rainforest streams. It has a leathery bill, its eyes and its nostrils are set on top of its head and its thick soft fur keeps out water. When a Platypus hunts for food underwater it closes its eyes and ears, but its bill picks up tiny electric signals from the bodies of the animals it eats. It stores its catch into cheek pouches and surfaces to eat. The female Platypus nests in a burrow dug into the stream bank. She lays two white eggs. Then, when they hatch, she feeds the babies on milk from patches on her belly.

▲ *Platypus swimming*　　　　　▶ *Platypus on the stream bank*

KING

▲ *King-Parrot*

Like all parrots and cockatoos, King-Parrots have curved bills with sharp points. They eat seeds and fruit. When they fly, these magnificent parrots make a loud call. In the nesting season, a pair of King-Parrots finds a tree hollow to use as a nest. After the female lays white eggs, the parents take turns to sit on them to keep them warm until they hatch. The parents carry food to their chicks and feed them beak-to-beak until their feathers are grown and they can fly from the nest and feed themselves.

▲ *King-Parrot*
▶ *King-Parrot*

PARROT

INDEX

Steve Parish has recorded Australia, its wildlife and its people with his cameras for many years. His first magnificent photographs were taken underwater and since then he has travelled the continent in a never-ending journey of discovery. Steve's aim is to show people the marvels that exist in this long-isolated continent, with its unique and beautiful landscapes, plants and animals. He feels that young readers, with their active curiosity and immense fascination with living creatures, deserve to learn about nature in the best possible pictures and words. Steve and his wife and partner Jan hope to inspire a passion for Australia and its wildlife in the readers of all ages who enjoy books produced by Steve Parish Publishing Pty Ltd.

PRODUCTION DETAILS
Photography - Steve Parish
Text - Pat Slater, Steve Parish Publishing
Design and artwork - Leanne Stanley, Steve Parish Publishing

Printed in Australia - Fergies
Binding - Podlich Enterprises

First published in Australia by Steve Parish Publishing Pty Ltd
PO Box 2160 Fortitude Valley BC Queensland 4006
© Copyright photography and text Steve Parish Publishing Pty Ltd

National Library of Australia cataloguing in publication data:
Parish, Steve. Slater, Pat
ISBN 1875932 20 8
1. Photography - Australia
2. Title - Big Picture Book of Australian Rainforest